Kuda
meets the
Buddha

Written and Illustrated by
Connie Southwell

Balboa Press books may be ordered through booksellers or by contacting:

Balboa Press
A Division of Hay House
1663 Liberty Drive
Bloomington, IN 47403
www.balboapress.com
1 (877) 407-4847

ISBN: 978-1-5043-9430-7 (sc)
ISBN: 978-1-5043-9431-4 (e)

Library of Congress Control Number: 2017919266

Print information available on the last page.

Balboa Press rev. date: 01/22/2018

BALBOA.
PRESS
A DIVISION OF HAY HOUSE

Dedication

This book is dedicated to the memory of my loving mother Anita who inspired me to be an artist; to my own sisters and brothers…Debbie, Cindy, Bruce and Grant, my many kind friends from all over the world; and most of all to the Divine in everyone and everything.

There once was a wild Balinese pony named Kuda who decided he needed a trip to go find the Buddha.

Who is the Buddha, you may ask? He is a man that is wise and will give you answers to your questions if you are open to his suggestions.

Kuda traveled through a dark green Bali jungle forest...

...where he met a monkey sitting on a tree. "Can you help me? I have a question for a man called the Buddha, and my name just happens to be Kuda."

The monkey gave a loud laugh and then thought for a moment, how to tell young Kuda that the Buddha simply did not exist!

"The Buddha", said the monkey, "is something inside of you that is wise and strong and knows just what to do."

Kuda was confused and thought for a moment or two, and then Kuda actually knew what to do.

All of my answers are inside of me, and if you listen you can actually see...life is about loving yourself and others, all of your friends, sisters and brothers.

This incredible thought made Kuda so happy and free, he danced a fine jig under a Bali palm tree!

On his way home Kuda started singing a song, he was so happy he knew all along.

I will always be kind and good to myself and to others, all of my friends, sisters and brothers!

Bali
Magnificent
Magical
Muse

The End

Printed in the United States
By Bookmasters